The Awakening of Kate Chopin

by Rosary Hartel O'Neill

A SAMUEL FRENCH ACTING EDITION

SAMUEL FRENCH

FOUNDED 1830

NEW YORK HOLLYWOOD LONDON TORONTO

SAMUELFRENCH.COM

ISBN 978-0-573-69774-6   Printed in U.S.A.   #3174

MUSIC USE NOTE

IMPORTANT BILLING AND CREDIT
REQUIREMENTS

CHARACTERS

KATE CHOPIN – 32, dark-haired Irish beauty, with waves and curls about her shoulders. She has direct eyes that look right at you and a captivating face with a frankness of expression.

OSCAR CHOPIN – 39, her husband, an aristocratic cotton merchant recuperating from "malaria." Handsome eyes, a feverish glance. He retreats into silence and heavy brooding.

MARIA NORMAND DELOUCHE – 26, Cuban vixen with broad smiling mouth, tip-tilted nose and full figure. She wears Spanish mantillas and flowers draped over her curly hair.

ALBERT SAMPITE – 38, wealthy planter with charm and animalism. Devilishly good-looking, deep eyes with an insolent manner.

OFFSTAGE: **KATE'S FOUR SONS** ages 11 and under, and her **INFANT GIRL**.

SETTING

The Chopin plantation in Cloutierville, Louisiana, a one-street town blighted by the Civil War.

Scene One: Six p.m. on a dreary Friday, December 5, 1882. The sun sets on shabby genteel furniture in a gloomy parlor.

Scene Two: Later the same night, December 5, 1882, Albert Sampité enters.

Scene Three: Later the same night, December 5, 1882, Kate's parlor.

Scene Four: 2:00 a.m. in the wee hours of the morning, December 6, 1882.

Scene Five: Same night, 2:30 a.m., December 6, 1882, continuous with previous scene.

Scene Six: Six days later, December 12, 1882, dusk.

Scene Seven: Several hours later, December 12, 1882.

Scene Eight: A week later, December 19, 1882, late afternoon.

Scene Nine: Five months later, May 19, 1882, noon.

Scene Ten: Several weeks later, June 10, 1882, suppertime.

ACT ONE

SCENE ONE

(Six p.m. on a dreary Friday, December 5, 1884. The sun sets on shabby genteel furniture in a gloomy parlor. **KATE CHOPIN** *enters in a glamorous robe; she turns up an oil lamp of clear glass with an amethyst tinge. Retrieving pencils and her manuscript from inside a walnut drawer, she makes sure she is alone, pours tea and prepares to write. Someone knocks at the door and hollers, "There's a beggar outside."* **KATE** *stuffs the manuscript under a cushion, hands money through the door, gets the manuscript and returns to writing. A jangle of carriage bells. Christmas carolers sing off-key. Then, a pounding at the door and a cry, "The tax collector is here." Children's cries offstage.* **KATE** *hides the manuscript, but an end sticks out. She trips over a toy, unlocks the door, exits. Outside bells jangle as a carriage arrives.)*

*(***OSCAR CHOPIN** *enters the room. He starts to change into a patched cashmere sweater, and is startled to see* **KATE***'s manuscript. He scans the manuscript. A noise offstage.* **OSCAR** *hides the manuscript.* **KATE** *reenters with books wrapped in gold paper singing something like -)*

KATE. "Oh Holy Night. The stars are brightly shining. It is—The night of our dear—"

OSCAR. "Savior's birth." *(***OSCAR** *kisses her)*

KATE. We're not starting that.

OSCAR. Why not?

KATE. 'Cause.

OSCAR. 'Cause what?

KATE. Your malaria could be contagious.

OSCAR. *(OSCAR looks at the gift books)* Karl Marx. "The Rise of the Working Class"—Friedrich Nietzsche?

KATE. They're for Christmas.

OSCAR. Darwin, the scientist who ate roaches?

KATE. They're controversial, but—

OSCAR. Radical.

KATE. Don't you want to stay current?

OSCAR. In Cloutierville *(pronounced "Clutchyvill"),* Louisiana? *Pas de tout.*

KATE. You said this respite was temporary. It's not even a town,

OSCAR and **KATE.** It's a place.

OSCAR. Look. I want to leave, too.

KATE. Living on one street with population three, I'm starting to talk to the birds.

OSCAR. I've several plots going to get us to—

KATE. When? I don't know how long I can maintain a jolly personality.

OSCAR. My brother and his wife want us to—

KATE. God-awful relatives conspiring against me. I want to talk about something besides—

OSCAR AND KATE. Their children and cooking.

OSCAR. I'm not going to feel bad because we can't afford luxuries. That's what I get—

KATE. The children can't go past grade school here—

OSCAR. For letting you visit your mother in St. Louis—

KATE. You're starting to contract, repeating the same phrases. Quoting your brother, Lamy, the dullest man in Louisiana.

OSCAR. Unfortunately, I don't have any relatives with intelligence.

KATE. You used to paint, recite poetry. Read one book for our salon of two. Darwin.

OSCAR. Cotton merchants don't want to read that "We come from apes" or "God is dead. We've been to his funeral."

KATE. I've got to have someone or something I can learn from.

OSCAR. I miss my watercolors, but sacrifices must be—

KATE. You said—We'd do something cultural, at least once a month.

OSCAR. And we will...soon. I like to read, but I also like to touch your face, neck, your breasts. *(OSCAR reaches for her.)*

KATE. Don't tickle. Let's move to St. Louis.

OSCAR. I'm checking your fatness factor. You always put on weight at your waist first.

KATE. My brain is shrinking, while my body expands. I can't be a writer here.

(OSCAR starts to undo her robe.)

OSCAR. If you don't like what I do, you can stop me quick enough. *(KATE reaches for a cigar.)* I did what you wanted. Took that god-awful cure, measured doses of quinine and hot mineral baths, treatments worse than malaria. I'm home three days, and you sneak out with your manuscript, that cigar in your mouth—up early! Up late! Always weary.

KATE. I've had to take on your role. We lost three calves this morning. Everything needs repair.

OSCAR. What was done while I was gone? Nothing?

(OFFSTAGE CHILD'S VOICE: "There's someone outside.")

OSCAR. Send them off. Our store was popular today—

KATE. 'Cause you're lenient—

OSCAR. Tomorrow no more buying on credit. *(He is suddenly nauseous)* Why is my body taking revenge on me? For defying the stock market crash—For believing in the infallibility of cotton.

(From offstage, we hear MARIA'S voice)

MARIA. Oscar, Kate.

OSCAR. That horrid woman with her wild stories.

KATE. She likes you.

OSCAR. Why not? I like myself. Everyone knows someone who's off. I wonder how off she is when I'm not there. Say I'm asleep.

KATE. Her father-in-law is your doctor.

OSCAR. Then what's she doing living in a shack, telling fortunes. They won't let her in Church.

KATE. Still her medicines make you feel better. And no one can top her with that sewing machine.

OSCAR. Remember your social status.

KATE. Phooey! She taught me to ride bareback, walk alone at midnight, smoke a cigar . . .

OSCAR. Those are assets? *(***OSCAR** *exits.)*

*(***MARIA NORMAND DELOUCHE** *rushes in with a large squashed dress box and a bag of medicines.)*

MARIA. Hi. Your dress got squashed. For a seamstress that's a debauchery. Doc says limit his quinine to once a day.

KATE. I did that, but he chases me.

MARIA. Good. Oscar's ordered you a walking costume. A high-feathered headdress.

KATE. Do my Tarot—

MARIA. Try this on. This isn't an ordinary gown, honey; it's an event.

KATE. I've no place for that!

MARIA. Wear the dress...and ask Oscar to hire me at your store.

KATE. Hasn't Sylvere found work?

MARIA. That skunk. I've aged five years for the one I've been married...

KATE. How can I function—all strung up? My breasts poke out everywhere.

MARIA. Nice.

KATE. Naughty. Oscar wants relations. He's barely been up a day.

MARIA. You're blessed with the gift of Venus. You evoke the goddess.

KATE. You can really grow to hate a person who worships you.

MARIA. I need to ask a personal question. *(Pause.)* Does Oscar have a big—You know?

KATE. When we were first married he was so proud. I can't discuss this—

MARIA. I must tell you a story.

KATE. Keep it clean.

MARIA. A portrait artist came through town and I wanted him to paint me, but he was expensive. I made a deal for this grand portrait, to let him bed me. And when it was done we had to— Arthur was four foot eleven. His member was— Then, he had this device from a Paris smut shop that made it even bigger. I said,

"Don't even think about that." *(Laughs)* Doc gave me a pill for Oscar for after the act. It reduces any fever caused by—

KATE. Whose idea was that?

MARIA. Accommodate Oscar. Once I'm in your store, I can —

KATE. Sex twice a day can irritate the malaria.

MARIA. Something my brother-in-law said— "Sometimes you have to feed the animal."

KATE. We've only done ten percent—of what Oscar.... He's thrown out his smutty tabloids—

MARIA. Why didn't he sell them—? .

KATE. He says he'd have done better in cotton if he hadn't sedated himself with spirits and sex.

MARIA. Lord, I used to do that. What if he worked in his uncle's bank in Saint Louis?

KATE. He's scared to leave the plantation... Unfasten this dress.

MARIA. Wait. An ingredient's missing. *(MARIA lays down Tarot cards on a black cloth)* Nine of wands—means a battle. Marriage card is reversed. You don't feel bonded—

KATE. I want to surrender to Oscar.

MARIA. That won't happen because of— your growing awareness of your own needs.

KATE. My needs include Oscar's.

11

MARIA. No, the cards that represent you are mourning and disappointment.

KATE. I want someone to give me strength.

(**MARIA** *turns over the emperor card.*)

MARIA. The man of your dreams is you. You are the emperor. Cut me a card.

KATE. Ace of wands.

MARIA. Some people read it as a big phallus. It means a new enterprise. This one's on fire.

KATE. Should I bed Oscar?

MARIA. Act like a slot machine. It gets men back because it pays off. Irregularly. Once every ten times or so. Talk to Oscar about my job. Flatter him. And promise to put money in the slot machine.

(**KATE** *exits.*)

SCENE TWO

(*ALBERT SAMPITÉ enters, pauses, opens a ledger.*)

MARIA. Albert! How's it going?

ALBERT. I never know.

MARIA. I've been visiting Kate hoping to see you—

ALBERT. Visit less.

MARIA. Oh, there's dust on your sleeve. I'll get it. You smell so woodsy.

ALBERT. You're in my light.

MARIA. How's your wife?

ALBERT. She exists; she's at home.

MARIA. Rumor says you're leaving Loca?

ALBERT. I try to maintain grace in disgraceful situations.

(*MARIA takes out a tape measure.*)

MARIA. Fine shirt. Blue on blue, like the sea. Soft smooth cotton.

ALBERT. Don't measure me.

MARIA. My dream is to make you an armoire of clothes. Silk jackets, ties, scarves.

ALBERT. No closer.

MARIA. I see you in town and you say you'll give me thirty seconds.

ALBERT. Don't touch.

MARIA. How can I fit that white suit I promised you? You said, if I made that suit, you'd wear it.

ALBERT. Three years ago.

MARIA. *(She puts his ledger aside.)* I still wear your locket. The heart with your name Sampité

ALBERT. Sans pitié means without pity.

MARIA. A lover is a puppeteer. You control my whole body.

ALBERT. *(Pantomimes a scissors)* Snip. Snip.

MARIA. The only addiction I have left is excitement and you fuel it in a big way.

ALBERT. Quiet.

MARIA. Oh, Albert, I remember everything you've ever done. Your tiny goodbye kisses brushing my hairline, curling the bow of my lips. Your moustache bristling on my mouth. I waited for you Thanksgiving. Sat up, eyes sleeping wide. "I'll be by later." That's what you promised. I slept by the gallery—so I'd be sure to spot you when you rode by—But you never came. I went by your place. You were sitting on your porch, feet propped up. Later I spied that flask by your side, and I knew why you were so friendly.

ALBERT. I'm through with heavy drinking.

*(MARIA exits. A few moments later, **KATE** enters in her red dress)*
14

ALBERT. I looked for you at the landing. Good, you weren't in that.

KATE. I've got to get ready for—

ALBERT. You look ready.

KATE. Living with boys, I've lost my sense of fashion. I can talk about playing ball and blackjack.

ALBERT. Put rouge on in front of me; I'll be a rapt audience.

KATE. Can I get you something?

ALBERT. Just your company.

KATE. Part of my job is to charm people.

ALBERT. I've noticed. Actually I'm here to balance the books. *(Points to some boxes)* Your inventory is low. I'd a shipment coming. So, I added on—fabric, seeds...

KATE. Last week it was harnesses... The week before, boots, saddles.

ALBERT. It'll put a few zeros in the books. I know with women you have to feel right to accept money. Men, we're excessive.

KATE. Oscar's unaware of the inventory you've supplied.

ALBERT. Good. I like the lightning bolt flashes that go off in my brain when I spoil you. It makes me feel I've a purpose. Money is the last bastion of sovereignty in this world. *(Takes her hand)*

KATE. Please remove your hand. You have beautiful hands.

(There is a noise offstage) Is that you, Oscar?

OSCAR. *(Offstage)* No.

KATE. *(She gets a roll of black fabric)* Your wife won't pick up the taffeta she ordered.

ALBERT. I don't see her. I live in the carriage house.

(ALBERT holds black fabric up opposite KATE's red dress.)

ALBERT. Gloomy fabric, next to red. Widow's weeds are all she wears.

KATE. I don't see why Loca wouldn't—

ALBERT. Appreciate me? I'm too blunt.

KATE. Coffee? Chocolates?

ALBERT. I put up with hopeless conversations, so I can visit the children.

KATE. Poor you.

ALBERT. I let her expound for five minutes and then I talk about something she can't relate to.

KATE. Why'd you marry her?

ALBERT. For a baby that later died. *(Pause)* I've a high need for freedom. *(Pause)* When the baby passed, I wouldn't let go of the dead thing. I got off my horse, crawled out on my land for hours and wept. A neighbor came along and thought I was dead.... I still feel guilty I can't love her.

KATE. She's agreed to the divorce?

ALBERT. Sure. If I give her everything. "I want the house, its contents and all the money you've got." That what she said. "Take them," I replied. It's like she's got so much, there's nothing left. False gods.... I'm just protecting the children. When I threaten to claim my half, she sets fire to the carriage house. Objects were never designed to replace the real anchors of life.

KATE. And what are they?

ALBERT. Friends like you. I'm happier about the divorce than I was about the marriage. What religion forbids divorce, if people are miserable and want to kill each other? We should torture our spouses for the Church? I've stayed married for two thousand years. Lived with a woman, blaming me for our dead children. She lost four out of six.

KATE. How did you get over it?

ALBERT. You never get over it. You get used to it. I spent too much time denying, clawing my way to sanity. Gave up warmth and companionship. Became a cowboy on the range; bucking and fighting... I rationalized coldness till it felt right to me. I work fifteen-hour days. Retreat here at night. I love my children, but I can't stay with her for them. Hour by hour a part of me dies.

KATE. You don't feel anything?

ALBERT. I do without. The servants say when I leave, Loca hums and sings.

KATE. But what do you want for your life?

ALBERT. To be selfish. When you're selfish you're true to yourself.

17

KATE. Is that all you want?

ALBERT. No, I want to be able to touch and hold someone. You've been in my dreams. The contents are blurry, but you're very real.... You don't understand the rules, but I do. I don't like shabby women. I'm embarrassed to be with them. It's the whole woman that's seductive, the way she moves, handles herself. It's not just the body. It's what's underneath too, the soul.

(OSCAR enters)

OSCAR. Albert, you look wonderful. *(They shake hands)* Magnifique. You always dress so well when others dress so poorly. *(Sees boxes)* More supplies? *Extraordinaire.*

ALBERT. And a get well gift.

OSCAR. You're the old style of Louisiana with "Let me comfort you."

ALBERT. I may go to Colorado—to buy land.

KATE. And leave us stranded —

OSCAR. *(Opening his Champagne gift)* Veuve Cliquot—A French monk discovered this—so it's bound to lift the spirits.

ALBERT. Have you read the paper?

OSCAR. My doctor told me I can have three drinks a day. That's down from eight. *(ALBERT holds up a paper with the headlines: 1884 Cotton Prices Plunge. Railroads Destroy Markets.")*

OSCAR. Not before we eat. For supper I only want white oysters, white grapes, and champagne.

ALBERT. Paper says, "Spending on cotton is like—"

KATE AND **OSCAR.** "Feeding a corpse."

ALBERT. I'm trying to keep y'all afloat—voluntarily—Look at these bills: binding: $1,045—cotton bagging: $5,450—bales: $1,970. We need to make some daring changes.

OSCAR. Not to worry. I don't pay bills until the last day they're due. I've got envelopes marked Tuesday, Wednesday, Thursday, Friday—and a bill in each slot.

ALBERT. What kind of business is this?

KATE. It's the business most people have now.

OSCAR. *(To* **KATE***)* But not Albert. He pays workers a pittance— fires them without pay and hires more for less money. Well, I can't let my workers starve. It could be me.

ALBERT. *(To* **OSCAR***)* It's going to be you.

KATE. Perhaps we should hire Marie Normand.

OSCAR. Good God. A woman like that doesn't come up the highway; she comes up an alley.

*(***ALBERT** *and* **OSCAR** *laugh incessantly.)*

ALBERT. *(To* **KATE***)* What do you know about her—?

OSCAR. She's absolutely no self-doubt. Now, Albert. What do you know?

ALBERT. She seems like a sweet soul, but I wouldn't get too close; she bites.

OSCAR. Every man in town will tell you something different.

KATE. *(To OSCAR)* One thing I hate is when I try to help and you call my suggestions ridiculous!

OSCAR. I'm doing the best I can without taking big risks. *(Laughs again)*

KATE. Maybe you should be daring and less of a dope. I read the papers. The plantations that have survived have taken risks, followed radical procedures. Now Albert's leaving, we can't numb ourselves with champagne and pretend we're not drowning here.

OSCAR. *(To ALBERT)* Pardon. Kate has no idea of her place in the household. She's aggressive. *Comme un tigre.* Excuse us.

(ALBERT takes his ledger and goes outside.)

KATE. *(To OSCAR)* Was that a call or a summons?

OSCAR. Keep your mouth closed if you know what's good for you.

(OSCAR squeezes her cheeks hard.)

KATE. I like saying uncomfortable things.

(KATE takes out a cigar)

OSCAR. This is my house.

KATE. I never know how truthful I'm going to be.

(KATE blows at OSCAR)

OSCAR. Don't smoke.

KATE. I'm not asking permission.

OSCAR. There will be consequences.

KATE. Like what?

OSCAR. No one understands why I put up with you. *(Shoves her)* Selfish bitch!

(She slaps him back. He reels, recovers.)

KATE. Strike one. *(She grabs her cigar and smokes.)* Someday women won't have to carry cigars to have an audience for their thoughts.

OSCAR. I'm just a businessman who wants a good life for his children and a happy wife. I'm not the enemy. *Je ne suis pas le diable.*

(He exits.)

KATE. Maybe all wives should wear black.

SCENE THREE

KATE's Parlor

(**ALBERT** returns.)

KATE. One day, I'll pull myself together and determine what character of woman I am.

ALBERT. Why bother when I can tell you who you are?

KATE. You should go.

ALBERT. Don't join the long list of wives done in by their husbands. Close this plantation store, diversify your crops, pay your debts.

KATE. The land's been in Oscar's family for years.

ALBERT. You feel by guarding these things you're holding on to your life. But you're not. When you die, the world goes through your house like a tornado.

KATE. I thought—once Oscar was home—our finances would improve.

ALBERT. You have to be strong enough to live simply... I'm driving a vehicle most people would call an eyesore. What I could show you slowly and thoroughly—.

KATE. What would you want in return?

ALBERT. To be the one man you can count on. Don't you want your perspective to soften towards the world?

KATE. Perhaps—No!

ALBERT. *Entre nous*, every time I give money away, I give my blood away—

KATE. You've never been broke. I need to harden—

ALBERT. My whole life, if I wanted something I'd to earn it. Only a fine line separated me from death and that was money. Money to me is freedom. If you don't have money in America, you're dust.

KATE. All our overdue amounts are not in that ledger. **OSCAR** forbids me to look at the others. *(**KATE** brings a box to **ALBERT**.)* But I look anyway. I suggested we auction off all our antiques, jewelry—

ALBERT. Good God. There are dozens of bills, going back... years.

KATE. What's that? What?

ALBERT. You've seven years of unpaid taxes. They're going to seize your land.

*(SOUND: The dinner bell rings. **KATE**'s boys shout offstage, "Time to eat. Yea!!")*

ALBERT. I'll be back. We'll deal with this.

*(**ALBERT** leaves. Offstage, the boys scream after him. It starts to rain.)*

*(**OSCAR** "appears" in a mustard-green robe.)*

OSCAR. Toys all over the house. Nurse is sleeping in a chair. I dare not inquire if you supervised cook. The roast is scorched, the vegetables poorly seasoned.

KATE. I don't mind a little scorched taste. *(Exits)*

OSCAR. *(Calling after her.)* But when the children don't eat.

(He pulls out her manuscript and falters as he scans it.)

OSCAR. *(Reads slowly)* "An indescribable oppression... filled her whole being with a vague anguish... She did not sit there inwardly upbraiding her husband lamenting at... the path, which they had taken."

(LIGHT: Lights Fade.)

SCENE FOUR

2:00 am the same day

(There is a knock at the door. **KATE** *interrupts her writing and turns up the lamp.)*

ALBERT. *(Offstage)* I sprained my ankle. Riding those muddy banks. *(***ALBERT** *limps in.)* I exhaust myself so when I put my feet up, I'll pass out.

KATE. You can't do bills now. Oscar's in bed.

ALBERT. I tell my feet to leave but they freeze. See, I'm trying to go.

KATE. Right.

ALBERT. Why aren't you sleeping?

KATE. Sometimes I... get up too early and stay up too late...

ALBERT. To do what?

KATE. If something bothers me, I write. I stay with it till I'm strong, or the quiet hushes me, or my body claims the night.

ALBERT. Why?

KATE. Writing is my way to grow. Sorry. I have this deep, dark, dying contessa thing.

ALBERT. You don't have to apologize. I know what it's like to be lonely. I wish I didn't. You don't have to be embarrassed.

KATE. I don't require many people to make me happy, just some. *(Pause)* I'll wrap your ankle.

ALBERT. I'm forced to work, but here you could become isolated totally.

KATE. I know. I fantasize a lot. I used to picture myself as an Indian goddess floating above a waterfall—And my lover would glide to me, and we'd make love in the grass by the creek. And the birds would sing. And I would write all these wonderful stories.

ALBERT. Inside your heart and mind, that's who you are.

KATE. I rarely speak like this—Usually Oscar and I discuss his childhood, his work, and his health problems.

ALBERT. What do you want to talk about?

KATE. What's ideal? The reasons for existence. Our behaviors.

ALBERT. Our behaviors? When I was twenty, I'd have admired you. I was a roamer. I rode 'round the country, a satchel on my back.

KATE. I'd have fallen for you, I bet.

ALBERT. I tripped because I was doing something I shouldn't: coming to your house.

KATE. Is that wrong?

ALBERT. I caused myself pain to dispel other thoughts which... aren't good either.

KATE. You're talking yourself out of your feelings?

ALBERT. Towards you? At least halfway. I need to occupy my mind with something besides our friendship. We're meeting every day but not getting together.

KATE. In the summer, these issues will get pushed aside.

ALBERT. *(Laughs)* Right. This wrap feels tight. Can you loosen it? That's better.

(SOUND: Offstage noises are heard.)

ALBERT. Tell me about your writing.

KATE. Women don't get published.

ALBERT. Pshaw! Find out what the men did and do that...

KATE. I want to tell the stories of people who are disenfranchised, and—to be a Southern writer is already to be discounted.

ALBERT. Some people create better from a position of exile.

KATE. Not me. I want to be read.

ALBERT. Then you will be. I spent my life asking questions of successful people.

KATE. What did you learn?

ALBERT. There are no guarantees other than do your best, and most of the time it works.

KATE. I threaten men.

ALBERT. Good. You walk the earth with a voice that needs to be let out. Read something—I want to hear the words when you say them.

KATE. *(Reads fast from "The Awakening".)* "He stood close to her, and the effrontery in his eyes repelled the old, vanishing—"

ALBERT. To me. Let me... get it all.

KATE. *(Reads slowly)* "He stood close to her, and the effrontery in his eyes repelled the old, vanishing self in her. Yet drew all her awakening sensuousness."

ALBERT. Go on!

KATE. "He saw enough in her face to impel him to take her hand—And hold it while he said his lingering good night."

ALBERT. That's first rate. Don't stop.

KATE. *(Reads; slides and microphone voices may augment the reading)* "The voices were not soothing that came to her: 'I don't like you.' She went on in a high, excited tone, attempting to draw away her hand. 'I'm sorry you don't like me,' Alcée said. 'I'm sorry I offended you. How have I offended you? What have I done? Can you forgive me?' And Alcée bent and pressed his lips upon her hand as if he wished never more to withdraw them."

(OSCAR, unobserved, appears in the doorway and observes them)

ALBERT. It's wonderful. Your words are romantic, human—And oh so radical. I hear you and—I live in a new realm—where you're very alive—

KATE. Please remove your—Your sweet rough fingers.

28

(**ALBERT** *strokes* **KATE**'s *cheek, leans over, kisses her, as* **OSCAR** *enters)*

SCENE FIVE

Same night, 2:30 a.m., December 6, 1884, continuous with previous scene.

OSCAR. It's so discouraging, the wife I do everything for, values so little my dignity.

(ALBERT rises, adjusts his sleeves, bumping into a table as he moves away. KATE pins up her disheveled hair, moves to the sofa's edge. OSCAR turns up the amethyst lamp. Outside a drizzle falls.)

OSCAR. I'd better close the curtains. Well, that explains the boxes filled with merchandise.

ALBERT. I tripped and hurt my ankle.

KATE. It was late. I was tired.

OSCAR. *(To KATE)* You vile, egotistical bitch.

ALBERT. Hold on.

OSCAR. *(To KATE)* My God, I could have you killed.

ALBERT. Easy.

OSCAR. *(To KATE)* You walk around in your robe.

KATE. Don't raise your voice.

OSCAR. If I want to, I'll scream. Damn it. You don't like the way I run things, leave— *(To ALBERT)* I should nail you to the wall. Where do you do it? Before the children? *(OSCAR takes a dueling pistol from a drawer)*

ALBERT. Give me the gun.

OSCAR. Yesterday, I saw you rest your hand on her arm— I excused it as friendship.

ALBERT. There are transgressions. This is not paradise.

OSCAR. *(Points gun at them both.)* I become emotionally tipsy, when things go radically wrong.

ALBERT. People fail.

OSCAR. Like seeing you here. That's radically wrong.

(ALBERT takes out a flask.)

OSCAR. I bought you that flask, had it engraved—I used to watch you work, insist you stay for dinner.

ALBERT. I was indifferent to the meal.

OSCAR. Till you saw my wife. Let's call the children. Let them see.

(OSCAR shoots at the ceiling, then aims at KATE. ALBERT grabs him, they wrestle. OSCAR retrieves the gun, backs off, pointing at his temple. He pulls the trigger... nothing happens.)

OSCAR. I'm discontinuing your services.

ALBERT. You can't fire a volunteer.

(OSCAR sits. ALBERT takes the gun, looks at KATE, exits.)

OSCAR. *(Calling after ALBERT)* Careful on that ankle.

(OSCAR picks at a box of chocolates.)

31

KATE. I was wrong.

OSCAR. Austrian chocolates from your mother. Incredibly priced— She can't give anything without flaunting the cost. Still trying to lure you to St. Louis... Maybe with Albert?

KATE. I fell prey to kindness.

OSCAR. No one's mistreating you. *(He takes out her manuscript and reads.)* "She liked the touch of Alcée's fingers on the page, and closed her eyes sensitively—"

KATE. Stop!

OSCAR. *(Reads)* "She only looked at him and smiled. His eyes were very near."

KATE. Don't!

OSCAR. *(Reads)* "They continued silently to look in each other's eyes."

KATE. I need to be cherished for some deeper self.

OSCAR. Well, behave better.

KATE. If you'd encourage me to open my heart.

OSCAR. That's not what you want.

KATE. We could narrow the gap between how we wish to live—

OSCAR. You want to humiliate me—

KATE. And how we're living. Don't you crave love that is more joyful?

OSCAR. You're incapable of that. *(OSCAR pulls out a box of family mementos.)* I look so gullible in this wedding portrait. And you with that virginal face.

KATE. That was Kate O'Flaherty's.

OSCAR. Albert's get-well card. It feels dirty. The children's picture—

KATE. With their... your mistress. How I've paced at night—To compensate for that blow of over-giving I experience with you. I made love with you after each episode to see if you could still perform. I'll bet that's how you got swamp fever—Frequenting mosquito-infested whore-houses. Swearing nothing's wrong with looking at nudes—if you don't do anything. Tell that to the betrayed wives who sleep alone.

OSCAR. You don't wish to be a good wife and mother. Fine.

KATE. I've been a good one for a dozen years. I may not be, for the next—I don't know who I am.

OSCAR. You're Kate Chopin. My wife.

KATE. Mama wanted me to be a scholar, now you desire a good wife and mother. I'm trying to perfect who I am at different stages. Nothing stays the same. Writing helps me clarify—what's happening—When I state my needs to write, you say they're foolish. I have to find my soul. Be a mother, sister, spouse to myself.

OSCAR. *(OSCAR picks up the manuscript)* Spouse? There is nothing about me in this manuscript. It's consumed with Alcée.

KATE. I rarely say everything I'm feeling. I take parts out.

OSCAR. *(Quotes)* "The effrontery in Alcée's eyes drew all her awakening sensuousness." It's so humiliating.

KATE. You lack the understanding that goes with acidity.

OSCAR. "Alcée or rather Albert took her hand and held it while he said his lingering good-night." *(OSCAR tears pages)*

KATE. Don't tear it!

OSCAR. Why write if it offends?

KATE. To save my mind... When—I see through ripped pages... bleeding mosaics of my life—And must face how little you value me.

OSCAR. Say every nasty thing you can. I loved you.

KATE. When I was young and flirtatious. But you dislike the mature me.

OSCAR. Believe what you will.

KATE. I haven't known what I wanted. I've been living in the confusion of others' needs. *(She flattens out pages and inserts them in her manuscript)* For twelve years, I put aside my writing whenever a child cried. And children cried all the time. I hoped finally to get a writing life started. Late but started. But, you've kept me pregnant—I didn't want this many children. Last time, I prayed God would spare the baby but kill the mother.

OSCAR. What a foul comment.

KATE. You've kept me moving. Magazine to Coliseum Street to Louisiana Avenue—

OSCAR. Each time to a more prestigious address—

KATE. With less money,

OSCAR. Such was my devotion. Now to a plantation.

KATE. In the sticks! Too much emphasis is placed on longevity as a sign of a good marriage. I have to feel you're heeding my needs.

OSCAR. You have six children—

KATE. I need to write. Darwin had ten children—and kept creating.

OSCAR. You're not Darwin.

KATE. Mama'll pay for extra help. If we move to St. Louis.

OSCAR. Females goading useless ambition—

KATE. In town, there are other women writing—

OSCAR. Just because you excelled at the convent.

KATE. Literary gatherings. I wouldn't feel so misplaced—

(OSCAR swoops up a box)

OSCAR. Your mother sent this shrine of your medals—

KATE. Women do better in all girls—

OSCAR. To remind me schools here are—inferior--Next she'll tell the children I flunked college and spent the night in a brothel. We are not moving to Saint Louis.

KATE. I don't want to admit failure, live off Mama.

35

OSCAR. Then don't talk about—! Just because you're the only surviving child doesn't mean-

KATE. Maybe your uncle would hire you at his bank.

OSCAR. You have to be everything—win everything¬-

KATE. We should sell... before we foreclose-

OSCAR. Know everything. It's this writing that has you confused and it'll worsen if your mother gets a hold of you. You know nothing of finance. You run off with your fool manuscript.

KATE. I feel compelled to tell my truth regardless of—. You think it's easy to close myself off. I've got to believe my story matters— because only I can tell it from a place of absolute passion.

OSCAR. You are going to be sued and lynched.

KATE. I've a right to express myself regardless—. I'm trying to speak from gentleness. I don't want to be vengeful—

OSCAR. You have maternal... marital duties—You need to write from a place that invites people in. Maybe you don't feel like most women. But you have to find that stance. It's called grace, balancing.

KATE. Personally I'm not gracious. The first time around--

OSCAR. You should show good things about the -

KATE. It takes drafts for me to get to kindness. It's true I'm interested in a thoughtful look at relationships. Maybe if you could find the brokenness in yourself, you could understand my dark side. I understand women have limited choices. But at what point do I stop making excuses for--

OSCAR. It's not a woman's concern. It's a "telling the truth concern."

KATE. I want to be free to be angry, to thrash around in the gore and still be a woman.

OSCAR. You'll rewrite this... Change yourself and this material— *(He squeezes her arm)* Or I'll plow your brains out. *(He shoves her into a wall.)*

KATE. Strike two—

(KATE grabs a knife from her boot)

KATE. Push me once more, and I'll leave you for dead.

(OSCAR exits, lights fade.)

SCENE SIX

Six days later, December 12, 1884, dusk.

(Thunder. Lightning. **MARIA** *enters with a bag of medicines. Not seeing* **OSCAR** *in the room, She curses loudly in Spanish, yelling after some men who are chasing her, coughing as if she has inhaled smoke.)*

OSCAR. Sometimes I'm not up to your blundering personality.

MARIA. How are you feeling?

OSCAR. All right.

MARIA. Only all right?

OSCAR. I don't want to brag. You come in like an animal. You don't close the door?

MARIA. There's a cyclone of catastrophe out there. You can't do enough to make up for it.

OSCAR. The whole town knows of the affair. **KATE's** locked in her room.

MARIA. Arsonists from the White League sit there, playing with smoke.

OSCAR. They have to be there to set the fire. That's what they'll do if Kate continues this—this—

MARIA. The townies won't let her get way with—

OSCAR. It's a childish love. A love without consummation.

MARIA. For now. You should take your children to your brother's—the ungrateful... whore!

OSCAR. I don't want those men to hurt her. I can hurt her but—

MARIA. Give her a taste of vinegar—instead of those long tears of compromise.

OSCAR. Shut up. I have multiple personalities and not one of them likes you.

(MARIA dances about seductively.)

MARIA. The most wonderful things are waiting on the other side.

OSCAR. I'm too old.

MARIA. *(Pats his tummy)* We all have these tummies. I look in the mirror and made my peace with it. Now I don't see it anymore. Eyes are temptation. You see it you buy it. After you say what for?

OSCAR. You're not what I need. You're one of the evil clique. You started stabbing your way up. Your husband just died. He was only 24. Of course you had to pretend you were sad. But inside you're saying "yes." *(Pause)* I'll never go back to your life. I'll throw everything away. Each of us has a ghost— worth escaping. Last time you painted me in such a black corner, all I could do was cut my way out the back side.

MARIA. People are coming into your life daily to help you be decisive.

OSCAR. I'm not an indecisive person. I've made too many mistakes to be that.

MARIA. Kate needs a confessor. She's a nun manqué'. A nun without the habit.

OSCAR. I knew when my wife painted the bedroom blue it was over.

MARIA. We are all afraid of being alone. For the right money, I could feign being beaten up and scare sense into Kate.

OSCAR. Do it. *(Hands her money. She puts bruises on her face while he talks)* I wish you had known Kate before. I used to spoil her with letters, occasional bunches of outrageous flowers. Our home was happy. There was the sense the house had seen things. It was a house that had eyes. She wasn't a mother. She was someone who had transformed to— *(Pause)* I've got to try not to care so much. I don't know how to function as a person who lives alone with meager belongings and bountiful fear. Over the years I have learned not to cry, but this time there will be no good reason.

MARIA. Stop whining and destroy her writing. That'll fix her.

OSCAR. No. Not yet.

MARIA. *(Handing him the medicine as he exits)* Herbs you sent for—. *(Calling to him)* Don't take too much quinine —*(MARIA exposes "painted on" bruises on her neck as* **KATE** *enters)*

KATE. What's wrong with your neck? Answer me.

MARIA. Gash of violence.

KATE. The White League?

MARIA. They've surrounded the house. Keep near Oscar —away from Albert—They'll hurt you too. All over town, men are loading guns, blaspheming, frightening women.

KATE. Have you seen Albert?

MARIA. No. He's defying everybody, gambling, drinking, riding stripped to the waist. I enjoyed time with him before you came—

KATE. You —when—you were married?

MARIA. He ripped me open. But that didn't stop my desire to have him.— *(She lays Tarot cards on a black cloth)* Ask a question. Only one. Two confuses the cards.

KATE. Should I choose to be with Albert under these sorry conditions?

MARIA. Such persistence. *(Holds out the deck)* Think of Albert and cut with your left hand. Good. Choose a card. Another. Another. Few more. *(MARIA lays out cards)* The traveler card. Ladies' men run in the Sampites.... Card of ruin. Albert rides at night to stop a plunging depression. He broods for days. See that blindfolded man by the sea? *(Points to a card)* Albert's sad because the screaming woman—There. She's lost her mind. See. He beats his wife.

KATE. He's divorcing.

MARIA. His second wife. Cut again. *(Lays out cards)* No union card. No marriage card. That's you. Solitaire—that means solace. But— you've got the money, the success, the jealousy card, and—oh, no. That devil in flames? It's a? Death card, and it's coming soon.

KATE. Oscar's dying?

MARIA. Portals are closing. With Albert.

(KATE crosses to her desk, and packs her writing supplies.)

41

KATE. I come from women who lived to their nineties, when most died in childbirth.

MARIA. You taking the children?

KATE. I've already buried my father and brothers— Great-great-grandma got the first legal separation, built an empire on the river. Great-grandma killed a Yank who assaulted me. Mama married a tyrant to save her siblings from starvation. She claimed her widowhood 'cause widows control their property and children, but wives don't. I've got to protect myself. Maintain my stamina. It's difficult when you come from the position of "me first" because everything you've been taught is "them first."

MARIA. Don't go mad. Talking like a waterfall—With no one listening.

KATE. Wrap these toy soldiers.

MARIA. If you're going to your mother's in St. Louis—

KATE. Metal men break so easily.

MARIA. Make sure... it's without Albert.

KATE. I like riding bareback, climbing trees, recklessly high.

MARIA. Oscar won't let you bring the children.

KATE. What's the next step down from rural Louisiana? I don't know but I'm not taking it.

MARIA. Your mother is sick.

KATE. Better to crawl back and—

MARIA. The children will miss their father.

KATE. I can't make Oscar the man he was—before I became myself—

MARIA. You said for better, for worse.

KATE. I'm giving the world the best I've got.

MARIA. For richer, for poorer, in sickness—

KATE. No one should stay in a bad marriage—

MARIA. It's good to be surrounded by love.

KATE. It's also good to be surrounded by yourself. It's not a matter of finding the right person; it's being the right person. A woman who goes scary places, brings life full circle, and finds redemption. Not a coward, talking into her hand, and apologizing. You bet I'm scared of going home and claiming that!

MARIA. You're so negative.

KATE. I like my "darks" and I'm not going to give my darks up!

*(SOUND: Horses' hooves, a neighing outside. **ALBERT**'s voice, "OSCAR.")*

MARIA. I'm off.

(LIGHTS: Lights fade.)

SCENE SEVEN

SEVERAL HOURS LATER

(**ALBERT** *enters. A few moments later,* **OSCAR** *enters.*)

ALBERT. Your keys and ledgers. I don't have to work sixteen hours a day anymore. I do, but I won't. Leaving. It's a triumph of will.

OSCAR. People disband.

ALBERT. For the amount of work you put in, there is usually some...

OSCAR. Speak up.

ALBERT. You took out the old French fort your papa gave you.

OSCAR. Just at Christmas. It wouldn't survive the year.

ALBERT. The infantry are missing.

OSCAR. Yes. You're right.

ALBERT. I suppose... well, have a fantastic life.

OSCAR. We've had an expansion of all these modifiers. You can't just have a nice day. You have to have a fantastic day. I'd like a nice day.

ALBERT. I should have left before. But I hoped to salvage something.

OSCAR. What, a twenty-year friendship? My wife—

ALBERT. Don't be sarcastic.

OSCAR. Sarcasm from the Greek to cut or tear out.

(Outside a drizzle falls)

Today, Kate and I will be married twelve-and-a-half years. My life is simple. I take the blows at work and recuperate in my room.

ALBERT. We used to fight over this red tin soldier. Remember? I wanted him on the watchtower. You wanted him at the gate.

OSCAR. What do you know about feelings?

ALBERT. Don't ask questions you wouldn't like the answer to.

OSCAR. I thought I was your most valuable friend, but only you were important to you.

ALBERT. We shared real truths between us.

OSCAR. And you ruined all that. *(Grabs his head as if in pain)*

ALBERT. What's wrong?

OSCAR. Nightmares. Arguments. When I ask Kate about our future, she says, "I've no plans to leave you."

ALBERT. Not because of me.

OSCAR. Liar. I've a penchant for summary. Get out.

ALBERT. I hoped you'd have cooled down—

OSCAR. If we don't talk long, I might. You took advantage of my illness, so you could have the excitement of my wife—Now, Kate's

45

tormented because of... Alcée. *(OSCAR gets manuscript and reads from it. KATE enters and overhears.)* "Amid the dusky and torturous outlines of flowers and foliage, there was her dear Alcée." *(Pause)* Alcée/Albert? Albert/Alcée?

KATE. I'm so grateful for the rain, which has freshened the room. *(To ALBERT)* Don't leave without a word of adieu.

ALBERT. Adieu.

OSCAR. *(Reads to both)* "Amid the dusky and torturous outlines of flowers and foliage, there was her dear Alcée."

(KATE takes manuscript from OSCAR and puts it on her desk.)

ALBERT. My coat is somewhere.

OSCAR. My wife's a cuddler.

KATE. No I'm not.

OSCAR. *(Meanly, pinching her)* See, when I stroke her cheek, she leans into my hand, like she's waiting for my touch!

KATE. No, I haven't.

OSCAR. Ah, she's crying!

KATE. I've a cold... I'm not so wounded I'm dripping with heaviness– *(Looking at ALBERT)* But finding someone who reaches out to you when you need kindness–Who's a survivor–Like I want to be—

OSCAR. Quiet. Bitch!

(Unseen by **ALBERT**, **OSCAR** *stomps on* **KATE***'s foot. She grabs a switch, and cracks the floor.)*

KATE. Awool!

*(***OSCAR** *starts for her. Moving between them,* **ALBERT** *hands* **OSCAR** *an envelope.)*

ALBERT. I wasn't sure I was going to give you this but—

OSCAR. What is it—? *(He opens the envelope and reads)* Oh my God. It can't be. *(To* **ALBERT***)* Your company paid my hospital—

KATE. Albert!

OSCAR. *(To* **KATE***)* He financed my cure.

ALBERT. Kate didn't know.

OSCAR. You're ganging up on me. *(To* **KATE***)* You'll have to pay Albert back.

ALBERT. *(To* **OSCAR***)* Where did you think the money came from? The birds? The sky?

OSCAR. The carpetbaggers, the underground, I didn't want to know.

KATE. *(To* **ALBERT***)* I'm moved, overwhelmed. We'll make it up to—.

ALBERT. I thought Oscar would be grateful, but he's not. *(To* **OSCAR***)* Well, are you?

OSCAR. I want you bloody out my life.

ALBERT. I'm exacting payment in January. Eight hundred dollars a month. *(Looks at* **KATE***)* I stepped out of bounds. Now I must step in.

OSCAR. *(Clutching his scalp, to* **KATE***)* Get my quinine. You put Albert up to this... you parasite... *(***KATE** *exits) (to* **ALBERT***)*... leech.

*(***ALBERT** *moves towards* **OSCAR** *just as* **OSCAR** *starts to collapse.* **ALBERT** *helps him sit.)*

OSCAR. I over-reacted— it's the malaria. I need more hot baths but - we can't afford... Afford. *(Laughs)* Funny. I thought **KATE**'s mother financed my cure. Tight-assed widow! How much do I owe you?... In all.

ALBERT. Let's talk after Christmas.

OSCAR. The Note says eight thousand dollars, but I know... *(He stops, looks around in fear and sees...)* My God. They're coming true.... The dead... everywhere. See them?

ALBERT. No.

OSCAR. I'm not dreaming... There he is! *(Points)* The archbishop... glowing like a golden triangle... floating towards me?

ALBERT. Where?

OSCAR. Shhh!. There!

ALBERT. Are there others?

OSCAR. *(Shakes head)* He's telling me... . He's slipping a gold sheath... on my little finger.

ALBERT. No.... It's just one of your nightmares.

OSCAR. Aaaah!!! They can't see well, but they can touch.

ALBERT. *(Reaches out to touch* **OSCAR***)* Sit back; you're shaking.

OSCAR. *(Recoils from* **ALBERT***) First* Kate. Now my wallet. *(Pause)* Albert, help me, please! I'm losing my mind. *(*OSCAR *thrusts the note into his mouth)*

ALBERT. *(Reaches for the note)* Don't eat that. *(*OSCAR *stops)* I'm cutting what you owe me in half. Repayment for ...

OSCAR. I'm losing my senses... *(To* **ALBERT***, sobbing)* I won't accept it. *(To the Archbishop)* I won't accept it!!

ALBERT. I'm not given to sham. I did, do find your wife attractive. Good-bye. You owe me nothing.

*(*ALBERT *exits.* OSCAR*'s sobs turn to laughter as he does a macabre dance.)*

OSCAR. *(Marches, dances, sings)* "When Oscar comes marching home again, hoorah, hoorah, When Oscar comes marching home again, hoorah, hoorah La-la-la-la-la, La-la-la-la-la, La-la-la-la-la, La-la-la-la-la, And we'll all be there when Oscar comes marching home." Kate! Come here, sweetheart.

*(*KATE *enters with brandy and quinine.)*

OSCAR. I should have gone on the stage. Enjoyed the fanfare, the curtain calls.

KATE. Should I call the doctor?

OSCAR. You kidding? I just earned eight thousand dollars.

KATE. Albert's gone?

OSCAR. He released the note. All his life men have circled Albert for money and I got it. *(Does a jig)* "When Oscar Comes Marching Home again, Hoorah, Hoorah, When Oscar Comes Marching Home Again, Hoorah, Hoorah. . ."

KATE. Why would he cancel—?

OSCAR. Maybe for you. Frenchmen are haunted by beautiful women. They eulogize them. Or maybe, he saw the ghost dance I've become. *(Laughs mockingly)* He has this immigrant innocence, which makes him believe in marriage and its possibilities.

KATE. Congratulations...

OSCAR. I regret any pain caused by my "perceived indifference."

KATE. Even harsh partnerships require consideration.

OSCAR. I love Kate because she is kind and—very strong. Because...

KATE. I'd like to hear why.

OSCAR. Because she likes chocolates, sitting by the lake—And displays the army fort I had as a boy. You know I love you. We were like cufflinks. First son would grab one and second son would grab the other. What do you want now?

KATE. My youth... No, a listener for my new thoughts.

OSCAR. I like the old you.

(KATE and OSCAR are silhouetted behind the curtain as if in memory. We hear their young voices.)

YOUNG KATE. Guess want I'm wearing? You need to know what I'm wearing to speculate about what I'm thinking.

YOUNG OSCAR. No time. The greatest collection of intellects are at the table since—

YOUNG KATE. Thomas Jefferson ate here alone... I bought six purses.

YOUNG OSCAR. Six purses?

YOUNG KATE. One is for my mother. We're sharing it so technically it's for me. *(Ripple of laughter)*

YOUNG OSCAR. Buy a dozen more. I got money. Deep inside, it flames within me. Kisses?

YOUNG KATE. Careful, my dress is so tight that if I swallow a raisin I'll pop. *(Whispers)* I like it best when we're naked.

LIGHTS: Lights become realistic again. We are in the present.

OSCAR. I love you.

KATE. Men say that when they've stopped. You loved me once. You haven't loved anyone for a long time. You're out of practice.

(OSCAR kisses KATE and sees her fingers are bare.)

OSCAR. Shush. Where are your rings?

51

(KATE pulls out her rings tightly wrapped in a handkerchief. OSCAR takes them, puts them in his shirt pocket and adds his to the others)

OSCAR. Let's pawn them — at least. I'm going to make it easier. Lamy will take you — to St. Louis— *(They say St. Louis together.)*

OSCAR. Every three months—

KATE. Are you serious?

OSCAR. Provided you... do something—

KATE. Anything.

OSCAR. Stop writing. It's destroying... Why not play piano, embroider, arrange flowers!

(KATE puts a cigar in her mouth. OSCAR grabs the manuscript)

OSCAR. *(OSCAR flicks through the manuscript. Sniffs. Reads.)* "She looked straight before her with a self-absorbed expression upon her face."

KATE. Don't!

OSCAR. "She felt no interest in anything about her. The street, the children, her husband." *(To KATE)* Nice.

KATE. It's a draft.

OSCAR. You want listeners for— *(Reads)* "The flowers growing there under her eyes were all part and parcel of an alien world— which had suddenly become antagonistic."

KATE. That's how I view it.

OSCAR. Thank God women don't get published.

KATE. I'll change my name. Would Amandine Aurore Lucille Barone have been published if she hadn't become...

OSCAR. George Sand.

KATE. Moved to Paris and befriended—Balzac, Liszt, and—

OSCAR. Frederic Chopin. I know.

KATE. Would George Eliot have been heard as Mary Ann Evans?

OSCAR. You don't have her talent.

KATE. I've writing more lately, trying to make sense of the palpitations I feel. In my dreams, I'm running barefoot down familiar streets, trying to get home.

OSCAR. Put your shoes on.

KATE. I'm falling down a well. *(She undoes her clothes)* We should rip off these petticoats and heels that encourage us to be dependent.

OSCAR. Have you lost your mind?

KATE. When I talk politely, no one listens. I don't know how long I can stay, partnered with my pencil, talking to a bird. I didn't realize how profoundly smart women are hated. When I was a girl and later when pregnant—

OSCAR. Stop....

KATE. I was encouraged to write, read, reflect.

OSCAR. Stop.... If you know what's—

KATE. First to win honors for Mama— Then to rest for the baby. When I study for myself, I'm punished.

OSCAR. Because... you torture others. *(Quotes)* "She felt no interest in the street, the children, her husband." How can you write that?

KATE. You exhaust me so you can enjoy your paper and brandy. One more baby, one more invoice, one more caller.

OSCAR. I can't think of one good thing you've done.

KATE. I kept us from bankruptcy when you—. Nursed the babies. Schooled the children.

OSCAR. Ta. Ta!

KATE. You're a terrible father.

OSCAR. That's a boldfaced lie.

KATE. You squandered our money—with false generosities. Mama's money's been saving us.

OSCAR. I'm supposed to enjoy your—this Alcée? I'll strike lines out.

(Grabs her manuscript)

KATE. I'm not going to discard my talents—

OSCAR. Lamy wants to have you committed!!

KATE. Lock my starving creative self in the basement, to languish without water or bread. I'll feed her like I did my children, watch her grow strong and proud. So many women have walked the earth; this very spot, and their stories have never been told. Because we've been trained to contain ourselves. We're lovely, silenced creatures, hummingbirds who settle for pink sugar water... I've been born in the wrong body at the wrong time!

OSCAR. I'm burning this!

KATE. No!

(He throws the manuscript in the fireplace. She dives for it.)

OSCAR. Get back—

KATE. Strike three!

(He shoves her aside, lights a match and burns the manuscript. **KATE** *seizes a poker and swings at* **OSCAR.** *They fight.)*

KATE. You're out!

(A boy screams, "Mama, Mama." Another door slams and more boys cry offstage. **KATE** *and* **OSCAR** *struggle.* **OSCAR** *staggers, seizing his chest in severe pain, and falls.)*

KATE. Oh, my God. What's wrong? Oscar? *(She listens for a heartbeat, shakes him)* Wake up. Talk to me. Mother of God! Oh, no. How quickly we leave the earth!

LIGHT: As the boys pound at the door, "Papa. Papa. What's wrong?" The lights fade.

SCENE EIGHT

A week later, December 19, 1884, late afternoon.

(It is raining. The room is draped in black: funeral wreaths, shrouded mirrors, pictures, and furniture. **KATE** *sits alone.)*

ALBERT. *(Offstage rings a bell)* Kate! Kate!

KATE. You can't come in. *(Hesitates)* Oscar's barely cold.

ALBERT. *(Enters)* I follow my feet, and they directed me here. You can't lock yourself up.

KATE. I can't find seventy-five dollars to pay for the mortician, so I'm in hiding—

ALBERT. Done.

KATE. You shouldn't have—

ALBERT. You look rough. *(He peruses her diary.)* May I?

KATE. Yes.

ALBERT. *(Reads)* "She let her hand lie listlessly, as though her thoughts were elsewhere—"

KATE. I'm not in my right mind. I wake after three hours— Creditors pounding at—

ALBERT. It'll take a few months—

KATE. Relatives grabbing things to sell—

ALBERT. For the shock to settle in.

56

KATE. You saw the obituary. A description is given of Oscar so you can experience him slightly alive.

ALBERT. I'll remove these wreaths—*(He takes down a funeral wreath)*

KATE. Black ribbon is an oxymoron.

ALBERT. The flowers are wilting.

KATE. They're changing colors. If it's too warm, four o'clocks reflect sunlight; too cold, they absorb it.

ALBERT. They've taken the children?

KATE. Temporarily, maybe forever. Lamy claims I drove Oscar to suicide. The man's—

ALBERT. An ass.

KATE. My children hate me.

ALBERT. I'm sorry I can't comfort you properly.

KATE. Please go.

ALBERT. You need someone to... hold you.

KATE. Get out!

ALBERT. I'm not leaving when you're in pain.

KATE. I've got to write these pawn shops—

ALBERT. You didn't kill Oscar.

KATE. See what heirlooms they'll buy.

ALBERT. Here's a copy of his will, and the extensive autopsy his relatives demanded. Oscar had forty grains of quinine in his bloodstream, four times the maximum dosage prescribed. He left his power of attorney to his brother, his body to science, and his debts to you.

KATE. *(Reads the will)* All our assets are mortgaged!! Twelve-thousand-dollar cash debt. Seven years taxes. Oh God.

ALBERT. Sit back. Breathe. Have you eaten anything?

KATE. No. There's no money for—

(ALBERT uncovers a basket.)

ALBERT. I decided to play the Southern gentleman. Here's some fresh bread—

KATE. I must prioritize these bills.

ALBERT. Chicken soup heals all. *(ALBERT hands her bread with jam.)* Your mother's coming?

KATE. No. Her health is failing. *(Voice breaking)* She can't travel— And I won't leave the children here. Or, let all foreclose.

ALBERT. Let me care for you.

KATE. Being taken care of is a temporary experience.

SOUND: A dove coos.

ALBERT. A mourning dove—You hear? I'm afraid to admit this—because I don't feel there is —

KATE. I trust you completely—actually I have from the first. But Oscar's debts are mine.

(ALBERT *reads slowly from The Awakening:)* "She sat once more upon the sofa beside Alcee. He had not stirred. She put her arms about his neck. 'Good-bye, my sweet Alcée. Tell me good-bye.' He kissed her with a degree of passion which had not before entered into his caress and strained her to him." Alcée is me, yes?

KATE. Yes.

(ALBERT *kisses her slowly, then passionately.)*

(LIGHTS: Lights Down.)

59

SCENE NINE

Five months later, May 19, 1884, noon

(MARIA enters dressed like a fortune teller, carrying a picnic basket.)

MARIA. I'm not here.

ALBERT. Speak up.

MARIA. I have no voice. You were my voice. Oh, Albert, a rush of memory raised from my feet to my heart soon as you appeared. Remember that day we ended up throwing off our clothes and jumping in the surf. When you left, I cried for two years without stopping. You weren't my boyfriend; you were part of my soul—

ALBERT. Vampire. Don't mess with me.

MARIA. Fine. I'll depower myself. Take my teeth out. I have an unbelievable gift of being mute. I brought you daffodils. They're so yellow; when you hold them, you see spring. I understand your limitations. *(Squeezes his cheek)* I don't expect you to be thoughtful.

ALBERT. Let's get this straight. This is my body, not yours.

MARIA. I'm obnoxious, I know. Afterwards you'll love it. I went shopping. *(She hands him two bottles of wine.)*

ALBERT. I knew there was going to be a surprise.

MARIA. One for you, one for me. Adulterers have to drink more. We're always uncertain. We have to have a drink in our hand. I'm going to feed you a good cake at least once a year and tell your fortune. *(Takes his hand.)* I can read dreams. It's my genie ring. Rub it.... Don't you dream?

60

ALBERT. I haven't had a nightmare since I moved out. Kate helped me beat back loneliness.

MARIA. You don't strike me as a person who'd let himself get too depressed.

ALBERT. I have my erratic moments.

MARIA. You're dragging Kate down. Louisiana law forbids marriage between adulterers.

ALBERT. She doesn't care about marriage.

MARIA. You should. There are two ways to do everything. Adultery is the wrong way. To marry Kate, you'll have to leave Cloutierville... forever.

ALBERT. I'll cut people out of my life before I cut Louisiana. I own half the state... How do you like being a widow?

MARIA. I'm alive, well, and meaner. I know how to manage money. We both need a change.

ALBERT. If I put my foot out the door, the wind may blow me away.

MARIA. I doubt it. You are a traveler. You know all the tricks to get out of town. Want to visit Colorado? *(Pause)* That's as close to a yes as I am going to get.

ALBERT. Are you free? *(Pause)* If not, how much do you cost?

(Pause... Lights out.)

SCENE TEN

Several weeks later, June 10, 1884, suppertime.

(KATE is glamorously dressed in lavender, writing. Wrapped gifts, candles in pairs; four o'clock flowers decorate the room. She daydreams.)

DREAM:

>**OSCAR.** *(Painting in a sand box. Sand falls in from the sky.)* It's wonderful up here, Kate. They keep pouring sand on top because there's a leak in the bottom. Even if the box is broken, it doesn't negate the spout.

>**KATE.** Where are you?

>**OSCAR.** Most things are unanswered so I'm back here with the bohemians. They rival each other in goodness. It's all blue here, like one endless sky. Been painting all day. I don't squeeze in. I take two spots. We are all so artistically motivated. I'll be the last person in the sand box, just like the captain doesn't' desert the ship. Today's my day. It's been a kind of secret day that only I can understand. The goodbyes from earth are coming at me hard and fast. You're the last. I'm setting you free, Kate— marry whomever you want. I want you to be happy. Never walk away from your cloud. Albert has an unbelievable gift of being reversible. But if you want him, let him appear. If you go looking for him, you'll never find him.

>**KATE.** How can I reach you? *(Bells toll in the distance)*

>**OSCAR.** Feed your soul. Nurture yourself.

(SOUND: Chimes fade into dinner bells. **OSCAR** *exits.* **KATE** *awakens.)*

BOYS OFFSTAGE. Take us riding, Uncle Albert. Please.

KATE. *(Calls offstage)* Get your baths, boys. Uncle Albert is tired.

ALBERT. *(Entering)* Now I'm a relative? *(Looks at the table)* What's all this?

KATE. Our six-month anniversary.

ALBERT. It's next week.

KATE. No, today.

ALBERT. You shouldn't have gone to so much... trouble. Listen, I've got good news. You've been officially named "tutrix" of your children.

KATE. Wonderful. Custody at last.

ALBERT. You can take them wherever you want. St. Louis, New Orleans, New York. How about a celebratory drink?

KATE. Well, I suppose I should have something.

ALBERT. *(Notices some papers on the bar)* What's this?

KATE. I held an auction, sold everything I could spare.

ALBERT. But you're running the plantation so skillfully.

KATE. I might be admired if I wasn't seeing someone else's husband.

ALBERT. Kate.

KATE. Yes, Albert.

ALBERT. This is Louisiana. Adulterers can't legally marry here.

KATE. Don't use that word.

ALBERT. I suppose we could pretend...

KATE. No one would believe we never had relations—

ALBERT. What if I swore we hadn't—?

KATE. Why would you lie?

ALBERT. It's the law.

KATE. Let's take a cottage on the Baltic Sea.

ALBERT. I can't leave Louisiana.

KATE. Elope to Paris. I wouldn't take advantage—

ALBERT. You'd be the first woman who hasn't.

KATE. Let's tell the world we're a pair.

ALBERT. I can't— When I think of a genuine relationship, with a woman who accepts me, I shudder. I've thought this through, many a black night. I've been alone / married for a long time. Uncertainty may be what attracts you–

KATE. I like who I am when I'm with you.

ALBERT. That scares me. I need to be honest—

KATE. Can't this wait till after supper? Open your gifts.

ALBERT. What you like about me has a dark side. But you'll grow stronger from these "pain bursts"—

KATE. Let's hold each other, not talk.

ALBERT. I can't step up to the bar. I can't marry you.

KATE. I never asked you to.

ALBERT. But you will, you should... for your sons, at least. I stand before this huge cliff and I'm... going to Colorado.

KATE. Colorado? *(Pause.)* We'll go, too.

ALBERT. I said I might need to see some land.

KATE. You can't leave now.

ALBERT. You're forbidding me?

KATE. I'm debt free but for how long?

ALBERT. I'll return.

KATE. If I thought this trip was a dream come true, I'd say hallelujah—

ALBERT. Back up. Say hallelujah. It's that important.

KATE. I thought your dream was with me.

ALBERT. It was... is.

KATE. Go on... leave! Monster.

ALBERT. Hit me. Hurt me, if you want. The truth hurts, but lies hurt worse. You acted with dignity. You deserve better.

(She takes off an ornament and ties back her hair.)

KATE. I probably thought of you four times for every once you thought of me.

ALBERT. Not true!

KATE. People said you were a loner, fickle, violent.

ALBERT. Lies.

KATE. You don't get that reputation without some transgression

ALBERT. I gave you my heart–at least to a point–Then you found a wall, one I set up.

KATE. You want to get back on the carousel. Go. Find some younger, simpler woman. No intellect there.

ALBERT. Maria says you do fine alone.

KATE. I made love with a man I hated so much; I had to take a four-hour bath.

ALBERT. You and I can continue to grow.

KATE. I told myself something good was coming. You were that brave thing.

ALBERT. Part of me loves you deeply, but a bigger part loves freedom more.

KATE. Whom will I count on?

ALBERT. Aren't you mostly happy with your own creative world?

KATE. You disgrace me with your ambivalence.

ALBERT. I've someone else to spend my life with...

KATE. Oh my God, don't tell me.

ALBERT. I do admire your loyalty.

KATE. Get out! I'm too strong for your world ... where spinelessness triumphs.

ALBERT. You should go to Saint Louis—

KATE. You can't pass a cat without stroking it.

ALBERT. Get the anger out.

KATE. Find some nitwit like... like—

*(***MARIA*** arrives at the door with her suitcase)*

KATE. It's Maria isn't it? —Oh my God. She drips magnetism. But, she's got a lot of tiger in her, a lot of pit bull.

(Grabs a whip, cracks the floor. **MARIA** *exits)*

(To **ALBERT***)* Go quick, leave. Get out. Before I stop you. Have pity and— Never come back. No matter how I cry. Or beg. Don't... call again. Have mercy on me. Leave my sight.

ALBERT. *(Calling back.)* And what will you do?

KATE. Take a ride with God.

(KATE turns away and **ALBERT** *walks out, when she turns back...)*

KATE. Lord, he's gone. He's really gone. I'll never see his face. No, not today or tomorrow. Or wake slow-eyed and touch his cheek. Knowing that skin goes all over his body.

I'll tell myself bad things about him. His drinking—Fill my mind with his cruelties; forget the sound of his voice. List in detail—his flaws. Then, maybe my eyes won't hurt; I won't have to gulp back sadness—

(She goes to the window.) Wind's picking up, violating the leaves. Clouds are turning brown as if grieving. Best to—Get out of the circle of his influence. In a small town, there's no place he hasn't been.

(Slowly awakening to herself.) I'll move into my aloneness. Is this the price for being a writer?

I'm in the hands of God but I'm also in the hands of myself.

(Remembers Saint Louis and her custody.) The universe is lining up in a big way for that!

(Calls out with sudden hope.) Boys! Boys! Get packed. We're moving. To... ah, St. Louis! Where Mama was a girl/scholar.

BOYS OFFSTAGE. *(Ringing dinner bell.)* We're leaving—for Grandma's?

KATE. You'll see great art, go to school—

BOYS OFFSTAGE. Yippee! Hooray!

68

KATE. *(Discovering her strength.)* And Mama's going to... write and write. No one will stop her. *(Holding back grief.)* And when she's tired, she'll write some more.

(KATE dances in a circle. We hear words from The Awakening that have a happy expectancy.)

ALBERT. "Don't go; don't go! Oh! Stay with me," he pleaded. "Why should you go? Stay with me, stay with me."

VOICE OF KATE. "I shall come back as soon as I can; I shall find you here," She buried her face in his neck and said good-bye again. Her seductive voice, together with his great love for her had enthralled his senses, had deprived him of every impulse but the longing to hold her and keep her."

END OF PLAY

APPENDIX

Replace Scene six with this scene with Town Hags: 8 women

TOTAL CAST: 10 women 2 men

SCENE SIX

Six days later, December 12, 1884 dusk.

(Thunder. Lightning. **MARIA** *enters with a bag of medicines, not seeing* **OSCAR** *in the room. She is cursing loudly in Spanish, yelling after eight women,* **HAGS** *who are chasing her.* **MARIA** *coughs as if she has inhaled smoke and pushes the* **HAGS** *out the door.)*

MARIA. Out girls!

OSCAR. *(Going to* **MARIA***)* Who are they?

MARIA. Town hags... Bad ones.

HAGS. *(Screaming through the door)* Kate! Get out, or they'll burn your house down.

OSCAR. Sometimes I'm not up to these blundering personalities.

MARIA. *(To* **OSCAR***)* How are you feeling? ...only all right?

OSCAR. I don't want to brag.

MARIA. Where's Kate?

OSCAR. In her room.

(Front door bursts open. **HAGS** *pour in. To* **HAGS***)*

OSCAR. You come in like animals. You don't knock on the door? Out!

(HAGS creep in and crawl about the room)

HAGS. *(Chanting)* There's catastrophe out there...The White League knows of the affair. Men are playing with smoke. Ready to set the fire. If Kate continues this—this—

OSCAR. It's a childish love . . . .

MARIA. Without consummation—

HAGS. For now!! *(To* **OSCAR***)* Take your children to your brothers'. The ungrateful . . . whore!

(Men yell outside! "Punish the bitch!")

OSCAR. *(To* **MARIA***)* I don't want those men to hurt her. I can hurt her but—

HAGS. Give her a taste of vinegar—Not tears of compromise

(HAGS dance about seductively)

HAGS. The most wonderful things are waiting on the other side. Eyes are temptation. You see it you buy it. *(Flirtatiously)* After you say what for?

OSCAR. That's not what I need. *(To* **MARIA***)* You're head of the evil click. Last time you painted me in such a black corner, all I could do was cut my way out the back side.

MARIA. Women want to help you be decisive.

OSCAR. I'm not an indecisive person. I've made too many mistakes to be an indecisive—

HAGS. Kate needs a confessor. She's a nun manqué'. A nun without the habit.

(Men yell outside! "Punish her!")

MARIA. For the right money I could feign being beaten up and scare sense into Kate.

OSCAR. Do it.

(Hands **MARIA** *money.* **HAGS** *puts bruises on her face while HE talks)*

OSCAR. I wish you had known Kate before. I used to spoil her with letters, occasional bunches of outrageous flowers. Our home was happy. There was the sense the house had seen things. It was a house that had eyes. She wasn't a mother. She was someone who had transformed to— There was no lying in her just beautiful gentleness. She had not yet departed to some far away interior place *(Pause)* I've got to try not to care so much. I don't know how to live alone with meager belongings and bountiful fear. Over the years I have learned not to cry, but this time there will be good reason.

MARIA AND HAGS. Stop whining and destroy her writing. That'll fix her good.

OSCAR. No. Not yet.

MARIA. *(Handing him the medicine as he exits)* Herbs you sent for—. *(Calling to him)* Don't take too much quinine –

(Outside men scream, "Kill the witch!" **MARIA** *exposes "painted on" bruises on her neck as* **KATE** *enters.)*

KATE. What's wrong with your neck? Why are these women here? Answer me.

HAGS. Gash of violence...The White League— Has surrounded your house.

MARIA. Keep near **OSCAR** —Away from **ALBERT**—

HAGS. Or, they'll hurt you bad. All over town—Men are loading guns... Blaspheming... Frightening women.

KATE. Have you seen Albert?

HAGS. He's defying everybody! Gambling . . .Drinking . . .Riding stripped to the waist.

MARIA. I enjoyed time with him before you came—

KATE. You —when—you were married?

MARIA. No. He was—

HAGS. And seeing other women. Didn't anyone tell you? He ripped her open. But that didn't stop her desire to have him.—

MARIA. (MARIA *lays Tarot cards on a black cloth*) Pick a card. Only one. Two confuses the cards.

KATE. Should I choose to be with Albert under these sorry conditions?

HAG # 1: Such persistence.

(**MARIA** *holds out the deck*)

MARIA. Think of Albert and cut with your left hand.

HAG # 2: Good.

MARIA. Choose a card.

HAG # 3. Another.

HAG # 4. Another.

HAG # 5. Few more.

*(***MARIA*** lays out the cards)*

MARIA. Traveler card. . .

HAG # 6. Ladies' men run in the Sampites. . . .

MARIA. Card of ruin. **ALBERT** rides at night to stop a plunging depression.

HAG # 7. He broods for days.

MARIA. See that blindfolded man by the sea? *(Points to a card)* Albert's sad because the screaming woman—There. She's lost her mind. See.

HAG #8. He beats his wife.

KATE. He's divorcing.

MARIA. His second wife.

HAGS. Cut again.

MARIA. *(Lays out the cards)* No union card. No marriage card.

HAGS. That's you. Solitaire—That means solace. But— you've got the money— The success—The jealousy card—And—oh, no. That devil in flames?

MARIA. It's a? Death card—And it's coming soon.

KATE. Oscar's dying?

HAGS. Portals are closing.

MARIA. With Albert.

(KATE crosses to her desk, and packs her writing supplies.)

KATE. I come from women who lived to their nineties when most died in childbirth. . . . I've already buried my father and brothers— Great-great-grandma got the first legal separation, built an empire on the river. Great-grandma killed a Yank who assaulted me. Mama married a tyrant to save her siblings from starvation. She claimed her widowhood 'cause widows control their property and children, but wives don't. I've got to protect myself. Maintain my stamina. It's difficult when you come from the position of "me first" because everything you've been taught is "them first."

HAGS. Don't go mad. Talking like a waterfall—With no one listening.

KATE. Wrap these toy soldiers—

MARIA. If you're going to your mother's–

KATE. Metal men break so easily.

MARIA. Make sure . . . it's without Albert!!!

75

KATE. I like riding bareback, climbing trees, recklessly high.

HAGS. Oscar won't let you bring the children.

KATE. What's the next step down from rural Louisiana? I don't know but I'm not taking it.

HAGS. You said for better, for worse—

KATE. I can't make Oscar the man he was—

HAGS. For richer, for poorer—

KATE. Before I became myself—

HAGS. In sickness—

KATE. No one should stay in a bad marriage—

HAGS. It's good to be surrounded by love.

KATE. It's also good to be surrounded by yourself. It's not a matter of finding the right person; it's being the right person. A woman who goes to scary places, brings life full circle, and finds redemption. Not a coward, talking into her hand, and apologizing. You bet I'm scared of going home to St. Louis and claiming that!

HAGS. You're so selfish! Spoiled!!

MARIA. Negative!!!

KATE. I like my "darks" and I'm not going to give my darks up!

(Horses' hooves, a neighing outside)

*(**ALBERT**'s voice, "Oscar.")*

76

MARIA. We're off.

(**MARIA** *hurries the* **HAGS** *out*)

(Lights fade.)

THE MUSICAL OF MUSICALS (THE MUSICAL!)
Music by Eric Rockwell
Lyrics by Joanne Bogart
Book by Eric Rockwell and Joanne Bogart

2m, 2f / Musical / Unit Set

The Musical of Musicals (The Musical!) is a musical about musicals! In this hilarious satire of musical theatre, one story becomes five delightful musicals, each written in the distinctive style of a different master of the form, from Rodgers and Hammerstein to Stephen Sondheim. The basic plot: June is an ingenue who can't pay the rent and is threatened by her evil landlord. Will the handsome leading man come to the rescue? The variations are: a Rodgers & Hammerstein version, set in Kansas in August, complete with a dream ballet; a Sondheim version, featuring the landlord as a tortured artistic genius who slashes the throats of his tenants in revenge for not appreciating his work; a Jerry Herman version, as a splashy star vehicle; an Andrew Lloyd Webber version, a rock musical with themes borrowed from Puccini; and a Kander & Ebb version, set in a speakeasy in Chicago. This comic valentine to musical theatre was the longest running show in the York Theatre Company's 35-year history before moving to Off-Broadway.

"Witty! Refreshing! Juicily! Merciless!"
- Michael Feingold, *Village Voice*

"A GIFT FROM THE MUSICAL THEATRE GODS!"
– *TalkinBroadway.com*

"Real Wit, Real Charm! Two Smart Writers and Four Winning Performers! You get the picture, it's GREAT FUN!"
- *The New York Times*

"Funny, charming and refreshing!
It hits its targets with sophisticated affection!"
- *New York Magazine*

SAMUELFRENCH.COM

TREASURE ISLAND
Ken Ludwig

All Groups / Adventure / 10m, 1f (doubling) / Areas
Based on the masterful adventure novel by Robert Louis Stevenson, *Treasure Island* is a stunning yarn of piracy on the tropical seas. It begins at an inn on the Devon coast of England in 1775 and quickly becomes an unforgettable tale of treachery and mayhem featuring a host of legendary swashbucklers including the dangerous Billy Bones (played unforgettably in the movies by Lionel Barrymore), the sinister two-timing Israel Hands, the brassy woman pirate Anne Bonney, and the hideous form of evil incarnate, Blind Pew. At the center of it all are Jim Hawkins, a 14-year-old boy who longs for adventure, and the infamous Long John Silver, who is a complex study of good and evil, perhaps the most famous hero-villain of all time. Silver is an unscrupulous buccaneer-rogue whose greedy quest for gold, coupled with his affection for Jim, cannot help but win the heart of every soul who has ever longed for romance, treasure and adventure.

THE OFFICE PLAYS
Two full length plays by Adam Bock

THE RECEPTIONIST
Comedy / 2m., 2f. Interior

At the start of a typical day in the Northeast Office, Beverly deals effortlessly with ringing phones and her colleague's romantic troubles. But the appearance of a charming rep from the Central Office disrupts the friendly routine. And as the true nature of the company's business becomes apparent, The Receptionist raises disquieting, provocative questions about the consequences of complicity with evil.

"...Mr. Bock's poisoned Post-it note of a play."
- New York Times

"Bock's intense initial focus on the routine goes to the heart of *The Receptionist's* pointed, painfully timely allegory... elliptical, provocative play..."
- Time Out New York

THE THUGS
Comedy / 2m, 6f / Interior

The Obie Award winning dark comedy about work, thunder and the mysterious things that are happening on the 9th floor of a big law firm. When a group of temps try to discover the secrets that lurk in the hidden crevices of their workplace, they realize they would rather believe in gossip and rumors than face dangerous realities.

"Bock starts you off giggling, but leaves you with a chill."
- Time Out New York

"... a delightfully paranoid little nightmare that is both more chillingly realistic and pointedly absurd than anything John Grisham ever dreamed up."
- New York Times

SAMUELFRENCH.COM